52 Drawing Prompts for Young Minds

2020 Edition

Written by Jaz Johnson

Edited by Jaz Johnson & Brandon Tate

Formatted by Jaz Johnson

Cover Design by Jaz Johnson

First paperback edition published January 1st, 2020.

ISBN: 978-1-951626-00-6 (e-book)

ISBN: 978-1-951626-01-3 (paperback)

Published by TC Studios LLC

www.TCStudiosHQ.com

Table Of Contents

Introductions

Hello! Welcome to our 2020 edition of *52 Drawing Prompts For Young Minds*. This book is going to get your creative mojo flowing and make you want to start drawing!

This book includes the following:

1. 52 drawing prompts in eight different mediums (a) and thirteen different themes (b).
    a. Pencil (P), Color Pencil (CP), Acrylic Paint (AP), Marker (M), Crayon (C), Gouache (G), Watercolor (W) Ink (I).
    b. People & Poses, Magic, Water, Animals, Light, Things, Plants, Places, Technology, Food, Sound, Supernatural, Comfort.
2. 13 drawing exercises – one for each theme.

How To Use Our Prompts

Each prompt will list a hypothetical situation and a few suggested mediums to draw with, as well as suggested paths you can take with the prompt. You are **not** required to draw with these mediums or use the brainstorming sections. **They are only suggestions.**

Some prompts talk about you, but you don't always have to draw yourself. You can make up a character, or characters to draw, too!

The goal is to illustrate something using the prompts provided.

Share Your Work & Tag Us

We would love to be able to see the amazing things you come up with!

To do that, all you have to do is post your work to Facebook, Instagram or Twitter and tag us **@PromptParty**. Use the hashtag **#PromptParty**. Then we'll be able to see and comment on them.

Submit To Our Anthologies

Would you like your work to be published? Kids and teens just like you are using our prompt books all across the country, and many of them are submitting their work to our annual anthology.

An anthology is a collection of work by many different people. Each year, we publish one with work that is made using our prompts.

Ten percent of each of our anthologies goes into helping communities like yours. This money goes towards public school donations, public library donations, and more. So, help your community out by getting more people involved!

For more details on our mission to give back to communities across the country, visit our website, www.TCStudiosHQ.com.

To submit your work to our anthology, please do the following:

- Ask your parent or guardian for permission/help.
- Send an email to submissions@tcstudioshq.com with the following:
  - **Subject Line:**
    - 52 Drawing Prompts Anthology Submission (2020)
  - **Body:**
    - First and last name. (or pen/artist name)
    - Participating school/library/bookstore/daycare/etc. (if any).
    - Which prompt you used and the medium you chose.
    - A brief bio about the artist (you!).
  - **Attachments:**
    - Attached work.
      - Attached as a **PNG**.
    - Attached signed publication form.
      - You can find this on our website.

Applicants to the 52 Drawing Prompts Anthology must be 17 years old or younger.

If you are selected, we will reach out to you to request more information.

For more information on our other anthologies and a guide on how to submit to them, visit our website, www.TCStuidiosHQ.com.

Check Out Our Work

Did you know that we also publish novels, comics, and other creative guides?

To find out more about everything we do, visit our website, www.TCStudiosHQ.com.

Chapter One: People & Poses.

#1 – Dancing ballerina. (P) (I) (G)

> **Brainstorm ...**
>
> - What kind of outfit do they have?
> - What kind of dance are they doing?

Drawing Exercise #1

Draw someone in a superhero pose.

#2 – Meditating monk. (CP) (P) (AP)

> ***Brainstorm ...***
>
> - Are they bald?
> - Are they wearing a robe?
>   - What kind?
> - Do they have on any jewelry?
> - Do they have any items around them?

You can share your work with us on Facebook, Instagram, and Twitter!

Tag us @PromptParty, or use #PromptParty.

We'd love to see what you come up with!

#3 – Running athlete. (C) (W) (M)

Brainstorm ...

- What kind of outfit are they wearing?
- What sport do they play?
- Is there a game happening?

Do you want your work published?

Ask for your parent or guardian's help in submitting
to our annual anthology!

You can find more information on our website,
www.TCStudiosHQ.com.

#4 – Crawling baby. (I) (W) (G)

> **Brainstorm ...**
>
> - Where are they going?
> - Are there any parents or siblings around?

Did you know?

We also have <u>writing prompt</u> books you can use!

You can find more information on our website,
www.TCStudiosHQ.com.

Chapter Two: Magic.

#5 – Potion bottle. (AP) (I) (C)

> **_Brainstorm ..._**
>
> - What kind of potion is it?
> - What shape is the bottle?
> - Is someone using or holding it?

Drawing Exercise #2

Create and draw a magical creature.

#6 – Witch or wizard. (P) (G) (CP)

> ***Brainstorm …***
>
> - Are they good or bad?
> - Do they have a wand?
> - What kind of outfit do they have?

Did you know?

Lots of kids are drawing amazing things using our drawing prompts! Want to see what others have done?

You can find more information on our website, www.TCStudiosHQ.com.

#7 – Magical wand. (C) (W) (M)

> ***Brainstorm …***
>
> - What color is it?
> - Is it made out of wood? Metal? Glass?
> - Does it have a design or pattern on it?

Did you know?

A percentage of every anthology sold goes towards helping communities like yours. This includes donations to charities, funding of scholarships, creating of programs, and more!

You can find more information on our website, www.TCStudiosHQ.com.

#8 – Spell scroll. (W) (P) (I)

> *Brainstorm …*
>
> - What kind of spell it?
> - Is the scroll old?
> - Is someone reading it?

Did you know?

In addition to our annual prompt anthologies, every year we have <u>themed</u> anthologies that you can also submit to!

You can find more information on our website, www.TCStudiosHQ.com.

Chapter Three: Water.

#9 – Mermaid. (W) (I) (AP)

> ***Brainstorm …***
>
> - Are they under water?
> - Do they have any fish friends?
> - What are they doing?

Drawing Exercise #3

Draw a glass of water.

#10 – Puddle. (C) (P) (CP)

Brainstorm …

- Is it big?
- Is someone playing it in?
- Is there an animal in it?

Looking for a challenge?

Try doing one of our prompts with your friend(s)!
See if you can create something together.

#11 – Fish tank. (CP) (G) (C)

Brainstorm …

- How many fish are there?
- What kind of fish are they?
- What else is in the fish tank?

Did you know?

We also publish novels and comics that you can read!

You can find more information on our website,
www.TCStudiosHQ.com.

#12 – Shipwreck. (I) (AP) (M)

> ***Brainstorm …***
>
> - Is it on land, or sea?
> - Are there pirates nearby?
> - What's on the ship?

Did you know?

We also have <u>writing prompt</u> books you can use!

You can find more information on our website,
www.TCStudiosHQ.com.

Chapter Four: Animals.

#13 – Favorite animal. (M) (CP) (I)

> ***Brainstorm …***
>
> - What kind of animal is it?
> - Can you keep it as a pet?
>   - If you can't, what would it be like if you could?

Drawing Exercise #4

Draw an animal with a pattern on its fur.

#14 – Magical creature. (G) (P) (AP)

> **Brainstorm ...**
>
> - Can it fly?
> - Does is live under water?
> - Can it breathe fire?
> - What does it look like?

Does your school or library use our books?

Ask your teacher or local librarian to participate in our annual anthology. Write something amazing with your friends!

You can find more information on our website, www.TCStudiosHQ.com.

#15 – Baby animal. (W) (M) (C)

> ***Brainstorm …***
>
> - Is its mother around?
> - What does it like to do?
> - Where is it?

Remember!

The listed mediums and brainstorming boxes are
only suggestions! We encourage you to do
whatever you want.

#16 – Wild animal. (CP) (I) (AP)

> ***Brainstorm …***
>
> - Where is it?
> - Is it hunting?
> - Is it being hunted?
> - Does it have a family?

Did you know?

We post daily writing & drawing prompts on our Social Medias for everyone to participate in.

Find us @PromptParty and use #PromptParty.

You can find more information on our website, www.TCStudiosHQ.com.

Chapter Five: Light.

#17 – Candle. (I) (CP) (P)

> **Brainstorm …**
>
> - Is it lit?
> - Is it in a jar?
> - What does it smell like?

Drawing Exercise #5

Draw a sunset or sunrise.

23

#18 – Flashlight. (M) (G) (C)

Brainstorm ...

- Is it on?
- How big is it?
- Is it pointed at something or someone?

Did you know?

In addition to posting daily on Social Media, we have daily interactive posts on our YouTube channel, Podcast, and Blog.

You can find more information on our website, www.TCStudiosHQ.com.

#19 – Campfire. (AP) (P) (I)

Brainstorm …

- How big is the fire?
- Is there anyone making smores?
- Is it keeping someone warm?

You can share your work with us on Facebook, Instagram, and Twitter!

Tag us @PromptParty, or use #PromptParty.

We'd love to see what you come up with!

#20 – Shooting star. (CP) (M) (G)

Brainstorm …

- Is there anyone watching it?
- Are they making a wish?
- Can you see it up in the night sky?

Do you want your work published?

Ask for your parent or guardian's help in submitting
to our annual anthology!

You can find more information on our website,
www.TCStudiosHQ.com.

Chapter Six: Things.

#21 – Your favorite thing to do. (P) (AP) (M)

Brainstorm ...

- What is it?
- Do you do it with anyone?
- How do you do it?

Drawing Exercise #6

Draw a group of 5 of your favorite things.

#22 – Things that you like. (I) (C) (CP)

Brainstorm …

- Are there a lot of them?
- What do you use them for?
- Where do you get them?

Looking for a challenge?

Try our other prompt books!

You can find more information on our website,
www.TCStudiosHQ.com.

#23 – Things that smell good. (G) (I) (P)

Brainstorm …

- Where can you find them?
- Can you make them?

Did you know?

We also have <u>writing prompt</u> books you can use!

You can find more information on our website, www.TCStudiosHQ.com.

29

#24 – Things that grow. (CP) (M) (AP)

> **_Brainstorm ..._**
>
> - Do they grow tall?
> - Are they colorful?
> - Can they talk or walk?

Did you know?

Lots of kids are drawing amazing things using our drawing prompts! Want to see what others have done?

You can find more information on our website, www.TCStudiosHQ.com.

Chapter Seven: Plants.

#25 – Carnivorous plants. (AP) (G) (I)

Brainstorm …

- What do they eat?
- Where do they grow?
- What do they look like?

Drawing Exercise #7

Draw a garden of your favorite plants.

#26 – Trees. (CP) (M) (P)

Brainstorm ...

- What lives in them?
- Where do they grow?
- What can you do with them?

Did you know?

A percentage of every anthology sold goes towards helping communities like yours. This includes donations to charities, funding of scholarships, creating of programs, and more!

You can find more information on our website, www.TCStudiosHQ.com.

#27 – Flowers. (C) (I) (G)

Brainstorm …

- What colors are they?
- What's your favorite kind?
- Where can you get them?

Does your school or library use our books?

Ask your teacher or local librarian to participate in our annual anthology. Write something amazing with your friends!

You can find more information on our website, www.TCStudiosHQ.com.

#28 – Succulents. (AP) (M) (CP)

> ### Brainstorm …
>
> - Are they potted or in the ground?
> - Are they healthy?
> - What kind are they?

Looking for a challenge?

Try doing one of our prompts with your friend(s)!
See if you can create something together.

Chapter Eight: Places.

#29 – Space. (CP) (AP) (M)

Brainstorm …

- Are there planets? Stars? Asteroids?
- Are there any astronauts exploring?
- Are there aliens?

Drawing Exercise #8

Draw a brochure to your favorite place.

#30 – Beach. (P) (AP) (G)

Brainstorm ...

- Are there people?
  - What are they doing?
- Is there any wildlife?

Remember!

The listed mediums and brainstorming boxes are
only suggestions! We encourage you to do
whatever you want.

#31 – Jungle. (I) (G) (C)

Brainstorm …

- What kind of animals are there?
- Is anyone exploring?
- What's the weather like?

Did you know?

We post daily writing & drawing prompts on our Social Medias for everyone to participate in.

Find us @PromptParty and use #PromptParty.

You can find more information on our website, www.TCStudiosHQ.com.

#32 – Desert. (M) (P) (CP)

Brainstorm …

- Is there an oasis?
- Are there any pyramids?
- What kind of animals are there?

Did you know?

In addition to posting daily on Social Media, we have daily interactive posts on our YouTube channel, Podcast, and Blog.

You can find more information on our website, www.TCStudiosHQ.com.

Chapter Nine: Technology.

#33 – Phone. (I) (G) (CP)

> ***Brainstorm …***
>
> - Is there someone on the phone?
> - What kind of phone is it?
> - Who are they talking to?

Drawing Exercise #9

Draw an advertisement for a new piece of
technology.

39

#34 – Computer. (M) (AP) (P)

Brainstorm ...

- Is it a desktop or a laptop?
- What's on the screen?

You can share your work with us on Facebook, Instagram, and Twitter!

Tag us @PromptParty, or use #PromptParty.

We'd love to see what you come up with!

#35 – Robot. (I) (C) (W)

> **_Brainstorm ..._**
>
> - Is it big or small?
> - Can it talk?
> - Does it look like a person or no?

Do you want your work published?

Ask for your parent or guardian's help in submitting
to our annual anthology!

You can find more information on our website,
www.TCStudiosHQ.com.

#36 – Machine. (CP) (P) (M)

Brainstorm ...

- What does it do?
- Does it need someone to operate it?
- What does it look like?

Did you know?

We also have <u>writing prompt</u> books you can use!

You can find more information on our website,
www.TCStudiosHQ.com.

Chapter Ten: Food.

#37 – Sushi. (AP) (W) (C)

> ### *Brainstorm ...*
>
> - What kind of sushi is it?
> - Is someone eating it?
> - Is it at a restaurant?

Drawing Exercise #10

Draw your favorite thing to eat.

#38 – Fruit. (G) (CP) (P)

Brainstorm …

- What kind of fruit is it?
- Where does it grow?
- How can it be eaten?

Did you know?

Lots of kids are drawing amazing things using our drawing prompts! Want to see what others have done?

You can find more information on our website, www.TCStudiosHQ.com.

#39 – Spicy. (I) (AP) (M)

Brainstorm ...

- What kind of food is spicy?
- What happens when you eat spicy food?

Did you know?

A percentage of every anthology sold goes towards helping communities like yours. This includes donations to charities, funding of scholarships, creating of programs, and more!

You can find more information on our website, www.TCStudiosHQ.com.

#40 – Sweet. (W) (G) (AP)

Brainstorm …

- What foods or candies are sweet?
- Where can you find them?

Did you know?

In addition to our annual prompt anthologies, every year we have <u>themed</u> anthologies that you can also submit to!

You can find more information on our website, www.TCStudiosHQ.com.

Chapter Eleven: Sound.

#41 – Music. (C) (P) (CP)

> ***Brainstorm …***
>
> - What genres of music are there?
> - Which do you like most?
> - What instruments are used in them?

Drawing Exercise #11

Draw something that is noisy.

47

#42 – Loud. (AP) (I) (M)

> **Brainstorm …**
>
> - Where are some loud places?
> - When are people loud?
> - What do people do when things are loud?

Does your school or library use our books?

Ask your teacher or local librarian to participate in our annual anthology. Write something amazing with your friends!

You can find more information on our website, www.TCStudiosHQ.com.

#43 – Whisper. (G) (W) (P)

> **_Brainstorm ..._**
>
> - When do you whisper?
> - Why do you whisper?

Looking for a challenge?

Try doing one of our prompts with your friend(s)!
See if you can create something together.

#44 – Singing. (M) (CP) (AP)

<table>
<tr><td>

Brainstorm ...

- What kinds of singing are there?
- Where do people sing?
- Why do people sing?

</td></tr>
</table>

Did you know?

We also publish novels and comics that you can read!

You can find more information on our website,
www.TCStudiosHQ.com.

Chapter Twelve: Supernatural.

#45 – Vampire. (I) (G) (W)

> **_Brainstorm …_**
>
> - Where do vampires live?
> - What do vampires do?
> - What do vampires look like?

Drawing Exercise #12

Draw yourself as a monster.

#46 – Monster. (CP) (AP) (C)

<table>
<tr><td>

Brainstorm …

- Where do monsters hide?
- What do monsters look like?
- What kinds of monsters are there?

</td></tr>
</table>

Remember!

The listed genres and brainstorming boxes are **only suggestions!** We encourage you to do whatever you want.

#47 – Werewolf. (P) (I) (G)

> **_Brainstorm ..._**
>
> - Where do werewolves live?
> - What do werewolves do?
> - What do they look like?

Did you know?

We post daily writing & drawing prompts on our Social Medias for everyone to participate in.

Find us @PromptParty and use #PromptParty.

You can find more information on our website, www.TCStudiosHQ.com.

#48 – Medusa. (W) (C) (AP)

Brainstorm …

- What kind of snakes are in Medusa's hair?
- How are they styled?

Did you know?

In addition to posting daily on Social Media, we have daily interactive posts on our YouTube channel, Podcast, and Blog.

You can find more information on our website, www.TCStudiosHQ.com.

Chapter Thirteen: Comfort.

#49 – Cuddling. (CP) (I) (G)

> **Brainstorm ...**
>
> - Who is cuddling?
> - Are they sleeping?
> - Are they watching TV? Playing Games?

Drawing Exercise #13

Draw something that relaxes you.

#50 – Soft. (C) (W) (AP)

<table>
<tr><td>

Brainstorm …

- What are some things that are soft?
  - What are they used for?

</td></tr>
</table>

You can share your work with us on Facebook, Instagram, and Twitter!

Tag us @PromptParty, or use #PromptParty.

We'd love to see what you come up with!

#51 – Relaxing. (P) (CP) (W)

Brainstorm …

- What do people do to relax?
- What are some items that are used?
- What are some places that are used?

Do you want your work published?

Ask for your parent or guardian's help in submitting
to our annual anthology!

You can find more information on our website,
www.TCStudiosHQ.com.

#52 – Meditation. (W) (AP) (I)

> *Brainstorm ...*
>
> - How do people meditate?
> - Why do people meditate?
> - Where to people meditate?

Looking for a challenge?

Try our other prompt books!

You can find more information on our website,
www.TCStudiosHQ.com.

Prompts By Medium

Pencil (P)

1. #1 – Dancing ballerina.
2. #2 – Meditating monk.
3. #6 – Witch or wizard.
4. #8 – Spell scroll.
5. #10 – Puddle.
6. #14 – Magical creature.
7. #17 – Candle.
8. #19 – Campfire.
9. #21 – Your favorite thing to do.
10. #23 – Things that smell good.
11. #26 – Trees.
12. #30 – Beach.
13. #32 – Desert.
14. #34 – Computer.
15. #36 – Machine.
16. #38 – Fruit.
17. #41 – Music.
18. #43 – Whisper.
19. #47 – Werewolf.
20. #51 – Relaxing.

Color Pencil (CP)

1. #2 – Meditating monk.
2. #6 – Witch or wizard.
3. #10 – Puddle.
4. #11 – Fish tank.
5. #13 – Favorite animal.
6. #16 – Wild animal.
7. #17 – Candle.

8. #20 – Shooting star.
9. #22 – Things that you like.
10. #24 – Things that grow.
11. #26 – Trees.
12. #28 – Succulents.
13. #29 – Space.
14. #32 – Desert.
15. #33 – Phone.
16. #36 – Machine.
17. #38 – Fruit.
18. #41 – Music.
19. #44 – Singing.
20. #46 – Monster.
21. #49 – Cuddling.
22. #51 – Relaxing.

Acrylic Paint (AP)

1. #2 – Meditating monk.
2. #5 – Potion bottle.
3. #9 – Mermaid.
4. #12 – Shipwreck.
5. #14 – Magical creature.
6. #16 – Wild animal.
7. #19 – Campfire.
8. #21 – Your favorite thing to do.
9. #24 – Things that grow.
10. #25 – Carnivorous plants.
11. #28 – Succulents.
12. #29 – Space.
13. #30 – Beach.
14. #34 – Computer.
15. #37 – Sushi.
16. #39 – Spicy.
17. #40 – Sweet.

18. #42 – Loud.
19. #44 – Singing.
20. #46 – Monster.
21. #48 – Medusa.
22. #50 – Soft.
23. #52 – Meditation.

Watercolor (W)

1. #3 – Running athlete.
2. #4 – Crawling baby.
3. #7 – Magical wand.
4. #8 – Spell scroll.
5. #9 – Mermaid.
6. #15 – Baby animal.
7. #35 – Robot.
8. #37 – Sushi.
9. #40 – Sweet.
10. #43 – Whisper.
11. #45 – Vampire.
12. #48 – Medusa.
13. #50 – Soft.
14. #51 – Relaxing.
15. #52 – Meditation.

Ink (I)

1. #1 – Dancing ballerina.
2. #4 – Crawling baby.
3. #5 – Potion bottle.
4. #8 – Spell scroll.
5. #9 – Mermaid.
6. #12 – Shipwreck.
7. #13 – Favorite animal.
8. #16 – Wild animal.
9. #17 – Candle.

10. #19 – Campfire.
11. #22 – Things that you like.
12. #23 – Things that smell good.
13. #25 – Carnivorous plants.
14. #27 – Flowers.
15. #31 – Jungle.
16. #33 – Phone.
17. #35 – Robot.
18. #39 – Spicy.
19. #42 – Loud.
20. #45 – Vampire.
21. #47 – Werewolf.
22. #49 – Cuddling.
23. #52 – Meditation.

Gouache (G)

1. #1 – Dancing ballerina.
2. #4 – Crawling baby.
3. #6 – Witch or wizard.
4. #11 – Fish tank.
5. #14 – Magical creature.
6. #18 – Flashlight.
7. #20 – Shooting star.
8. #23 – Things that smell good.
9. #25 – Carnivorous plants.
10. #27 – Flowers.
11. #30 – Beach.
12. #31 – Jungle.
13. #33 – Phone.
14. #38 – Fruit.
15. #40 – Sweet.
16. #43 – Whisper.
17. #45 – Vampire.
18. #47 – Werewolf.

19. #49 – Cuddling.

Marker (M)

1. #3 – Running athlete.
2. #7 – Magical wand.
3. #12 – Shipwreck.
4. #13 – Favorite animal.
5. #15 – Baby animal.
6. #18 – Flashlight.
7. #20 – Shooting star.
8. #21 – Your favorite thing to do.
9. #24 – Things that grow.
10. #26 – Trees.
11. #28 – Succulents.
12. #29 – Space.
13. #32 – Desert.
14. #34 – Computer.
15. #36 – Machine.
16. #39 – Spicy.
17. #42 – Loud.
18. #43 – Singing.

Crayon (C)

1. #3 – Running athlete.
2. #5 – Potion bottle.
3. #7 – Magical wand.
4. #10 – Puddle.
5. #11 – Fish tank.
6. #15 – Baby animal.
7. #18 – Flashlight.
8. #22 – Things that you like.
9. #27 – Flowers.
10. #31 – Jungle.
11. #35 – Robot.

12. #37 – Sushi.
13. #41 – Music.
14. #46 – Monster.
15. #48 – Medusa.
16. #50 – Soft.

Drawing Exercises

1. Draw someone in a superhero pose.
2. Create and draw a magical creature.
3. Draw a glass of water.
4. Draw an animal with a pattern on its fur.
5. Draw a sunset or sunrise.
6. Draw a group of 5 of your favorite things.
7. Draw a garden of your favorite plants.
8. Draw a brochure to your favorite place.
9. Draw an advertisement for a new piece of technology.
10. Draw your favorite thing to eat.
11. Draw something that is noisy.
12. Draw yourself as a monster.
13. Draw something that relaxes you.

Thank You!

That's all for now! We hope you had fun exploring your creative side! If you did, please considering leaving us a review. We'd really appreciate it!

You can come back next year for our 2021 edition and do a whole new set of prompts, and a new set of exercises.

But in the meantime, if you're looking for something to keep you busy, you can try our other prompt books:

- 52 Writing Prompts for Young Minds.
- 365 Drawing Prompts.
- 100 Character Prompts.
- And more!

And if you're looking for something fun to read to give you some inspiration, check out our fiction books and comics!

For more information, check out our website, www.TCStudiosHQ.com.